HOW TO PLA IN

Daily Guitar Lessons for Beginners

By Troy Nelson

G000295807

To download the companion audio files for this book, visit: www.troynelsonmusic.com/audio-downloads

ISBN 9781686421921   Copyright © 2019 Troy Nelson

International Copyright Secured. All Rights Reserved

INTRODUCTION

As someone who's new to the guitar, you've probably spent some time looking for the best method to help you learn the instrument—and there are tons of them on the market! Most guitar methods follow a similar lesson plan: they start with the different components of the guitar (neck, body, frets, bridge, etc.), move on to tuning the guitar, and then teach a few open chords and how to sight-read the first few notes on each string, and so on.

How To Play Guitar in 14 Days focuses on a few of these topics, as well, but what separates this method from the others is how quickly you'll be able to play something on the instrument—that is, something that sounds good! The goal of this method is to get you playing confidently—and sounding *good* while doing it—as fast as possible because frustration is arguably the No. 1 reason why budding guitarists quit. And what better way to alleviate frustration than by playing something that is relatively easy *and* sounds great?

So, how is this accomplished? Well, with an *open tuning*. The strings on the guitar are typically tuned E–A–D–G–B–E, low to high (ceiling to floor when holding the guitar in proper playing position). This is known as *standard tuning*. When the open strings are strummed together in standard tuning, without fretting any notes on the neck, the resultant sound is somewhat dissonant—certainly not something that would make your friends and family come running to hear you play. And it's the fretting part that gives beginners the most trouble. Strumming your thumb or pick through the six open strings is easy, but applying your fingers to the strings is another story. This is where the open tuning—in our case, Open E—comes into play.

By tuning your guitar to Open E tuning (low to high: E–B–E–G#–B–E), you are able to strum through all six open strings and produce a nice, consonant E major chord—no fretting necessary! This tuning also makes playing things like a blues shuffle easier than when in standard tuning. Open E tuning allows you to sound good *while* reducing the amount of fretting necessary to do so (this will become much clearer as you progress through the book). But we won't relegate ourselves to just open strings; we'll also learn to play chords and riffs that are common to this tuning. The benefit of this method is that you'll sound good while developing good guitar technique. In other words, you won't have to wait on your technique to make sweet-sounding music!

After one week of Open E tuning, we'll migrate to standard tuning and learn some of the same music examples that we learned in open tuning, among others. While Week 1 is primarily focused on pick-hand development, Week 2 goes heavy on the fret hand—the most challenging hand for beginners. Since standard tuning is the tuning of choice for most guitarists, we'll start to introduce some of the most common open chords, chord progressions, and scales. One topic that you typically find in other guitar methods but will *not* be covered in *How To Play Guitar in 14 Days* is note reading, or sight reading. While learning to read notes on the staff is certainly a noble endeavor, one that you might want to pursue in the future, the reality is that most guitar music today is presented in tab (short for "tablature") rather than standard notation.

The tab staff is comprised of six horizontal lines, each representing a string on the guitar. Numbers that appear on the lines/strings indicate which frets the notes are to be played on. The music examples in this book are presented exclusively in tab because this approach falls in line with the goal of getting you playing well in the least amount of time, and tab is easier to learn than standard notation. One other thing you won't see in this method is a breakdown of the various parts of the guitar. While that is certainly information you're going to want to know, you can easily find this stuff by doing a quick Google search.

How To Play Guitar in 14 Days is divided into 14 lessons, one for each day of the two-week program. Within each lesson/day are six "mini-lessons." The goal is to spend 15 minutes practicing the music exercises in each mini-lesson, for a total of 90 minutes (15 X 6 = 90) per day. The one exception is Day 14. On this day, the entire 90 minutes are devoted to a single musical example that acts as a review of the material presented during the two-week program.

As mentioned earlier, Week 1 focuses exclusively on Open E tuning. The objective here is to teach you guitar fundamentals without the frustrations that often arise when music doesn't sound the way you want it to. Think of this part of the book as a confidence booster before you encounter Week 2 and the challenges of standard tuning.

WEEK 1: OPEN E TUNING

Blues Shuffle

A blues shuffle in Open E tuning is about as easy as it gets—and it sounds great! In these mini-lessons, we'll explore several ways to play a shuffle in this tuning, building up your confidence one riff at a time!

Strumming

One of the most important—but often neglected—guitar techniques is chord strumming. Here, we'll mostly focus on rhythms and pick-hand techniques like upstrokes and downstrokes, saving fret-hand technique for Week 2, when more chords will be introduced.

Single-Note Picking

While strumming handles the majority of the chord work on guitar, single-note picking plays an important role, as well. Single-note picking takes considerable time to develop, so we'll spend both weeks working on this technique, applying it to the chords we learn along the way.

Fingerpicking

The sound of a fingerpicked passage being played on an acoustic guitar is hard to beat (it sounds darn good on electric guitar, too). In these mini-lessons, we're going to focus on articulating individual notes with the pick-hand fingers. Think of these lessons as the fingerpicked versions of the single-note-picking exercises.

Rests

Most guitarists are guilty of over-playing, including yours truly, because we lose sight of the fact that rests—those little moments of silence—are equally as important as the notes we are playing. Without these musical pauses, melodies lose their impact and the emotional effect they would otherwise have on the listener. In these lessons, we're going to learn how to respond to rests when we encounter them in music, and how they should be counted.

Technique

Like any instrument, the guitar requires the player to be equipped with several techniques in order to play it properly and effectively. Strumming and single-note picking are just a couple of the many techniques every guitarist should be well-versed in. We'll cover some of the most important ones here, including hammer-ones, pull-offs, slides, and palm muting, among others.

Week 2 turns our attention to standard tuning, with an emphasis on the fret hand. While some of the material is an extension of Week 1, much of it will be brand new to you.

WEEK 2: STANDARD TUNING

Blues Shuffle

The lessons in this section are a continuation of the shuffles we worked on in Week 1. Here, we'll learn how the change in tuning (from Open E to standard) requires a different approach in the fret hand. Regardless of which tuning is employed, shuffles always sound great!

Strumming

These mini-lessons expand upon the strumming exercises from Week 1. However, now that we're in standard tuning, the focus shifts to the fret hand and learning new, standard-tuned chord shapes. Changing between these chords is more difficult, but the Open E exercises from Week 1 should have us prepared for the challenge!

Single-Note Picking

This section is also a continuation of the lessons from Week 1. Although we'll work on exercises similar to the ones from the previous week, the technical challenges will be ratcheted up a notch because of the new (standard) tuning.

Fingerpicking

This collection of mini-lessons is also an extension of material that we covered in Week 1. Here, we'll apply the fingerpicking patterns that we learned in the previous week to standard-tuned chords.

Chord Progression

These mini-lessons are an opportunity to delve into some of the many chords available in standard tuning, including open chords, 7th chords, and barre chords. The common three- and four-chord progressions featured here also offer an opportunity to continue working on switching between chords while strumming.

Scale

In this section, we're going to explore the seven-note major and minor scales, as well as their five-note counterparts, major and minor pentatonic. While most guitar methods teach these scales in open position (i.e., patterns that contain open strings), we're going to learn them at fret 5, a more practical neck position.

DAY 14: PUTTING IT ALL TOGETHER

On the book's final day, we'll spend the entire 90-minute session practicing an eight-measure exercise that incorporates nearly all of the material that we've learned over the past two weeks, including chord strumming, single-note picking, and rests, as well as technical topics such as hammer-ons, pull-offs, slides, and chord muting. In addition to being a great way to review the material that we've covered, this example is also a great way to determine how far you've come in your playing and what areas need further development and refinement.

While much has been made of Open E tuning, it's really just the beginning of your journey toward guitar fluency in *standard tuning*. Sounding good in the early stages is important, but sticking with the program is the goal!

Finally, I'd be remiss if I didn't touch on the electric versus acoustic debate. While beginning on acoustic guitar has been advocated for decades by many guitar teachers, I'm actually in favor of students starting on electric because it's easier to play. That said, both types have their benefits, and both will work just fine for the music exercises in this book. Choose whichever instrument works best for you!

Best of luck in your guitar studies!

Troy Nelson

HOW TO USE THIS BOOK

Granted, 90 minutes of practice per day can seem daunting—and that's OK! Just because the book is structured to teach you guitar in 14 days doesn't mean you have to follow the program precisely. On the contrary, if you have, say, 30 minutes to devote to the book each day, then simply extend each lesson (day) to a three-day practice session. The material is there for you to use, whether you get through the book in 14 days or 40.

While the 14-day plan is the goal, it's probably unrealistic for some. The important thing is to stick with it because the material in this book will have you playing guitar fluently and confidently. How quickly just depends on the amount of time you're able to spend on getting there.

Before you begin your daily sessions, however, I suggest spending 10–15 minutes listening to the accompanying audio to get a feel for the forthcoming exercises, as well as reading through each section's introductory material to better understand what you're about to learn. That way, you can spend the *full* 90 minutes (or however much time you have to practice that day) playing the music examples.

To help keep you on track in your practice sessions, time codes are included throughout the book. Simply set the timer on your smart phone to 90 minutes (1:30) and move on to the next mini-lesson every 15 minutes. Or, you can set the timer to 15 minutes (0:15) and move on to the next lesson when the timer goes off, repeating this step for every new lesson.

Next, set your metronome (or drum loop, click track, etc.) to a tempo at which you can play the exercise all the way through without making too many mistakes (40–50 beats per minute is probably a good starting point for most exercises). Once you're able to play the exercise cleanly, increase your tempo by 4–5 BPM. Again, make sure you can play through the exercise without making too many mistakes. If the speed is too fast, back off a bit until your execution is precise. Continue to increase your tempo incrementally until it's time to move on to the next section.

There will be times when the timer goes off and you feel like you didn't adequately learn the material. When this happens, I suggest moving on to the next section nonetheless. It may seem counterintuitive, but it's better to continue progressing through the book than to extend the practice time in order to perfect the material. After you've completed the book, you can always go back and review the exercises. In fact, I recommend it. Making steady progress, while not always perfectly, keeps you mentally sharp and motived. Focusing too much on any one exercise is a sure way to sidetrack your sessions.

Lastly—and this is important—if you ever feel yourself getting physically fatigued or pain develops in any part of your body, especially your hands or arms, immediately take a break until the discomfort subsides, whether it's for 10 minutes, an hour, or for the rest of the day. You never want to push yourself beyond your physical limits and cause permanent damage. As mentioned earlier, the material isn't going anywhere; you can always go back to it when you're feeling 100%.

TUNING METHODS

Before we get into Open E tuning, let's first get acclimated to tuning the strings to standard tuning: E–A–D–G–B–E (low to high). Standard tuning is far and away the most popular tuning for guitar, and there are several ways to go about tuning the instrument.

TUNING APPS

For beginners, the easiest way to tune the guitar is to download a free guitar-tuner app to your smart phone. Most work well, but let the star ratings help you decide.

Once you have the tuner app downloaded to your phone, simply pluck each string individually while adjusting its corresponding tuning peg until you reach the desired pitch. The tuner will indicate whether the string is above (sharp) or below (flat) the desired pitch. Loosening the string lowers the pitch, and tightening the string raises the pitch.

Start with string 6, the low E string (standard tuning contains *two* E strings), which is the thickest of the six strings (and closest to the ceiling). While adjusting the tension, pay strict attention to the slack in the string. If it becomes too loose or too taut, you'll need to turn the tuning peg in the opposite direction. Let the tuner be your guide, but the string's tension (or lack thereof) will also let you know if you're heading in the right direction. After you get the low E string to pitch, work your way through strings 5–1 in the same manner. Newer strings tend to go out of tune more frequently than worn strings, so you'll need to tune up more frequently if your guitar has a fresh set.

Some apps have tuning tutorials for beginners, as well as chromatic and instrument-specific tuning options such as standard, Open G, and… yes, Open E.

ELECTRONIC TUNERS

Although many electronic tuners have seen their popularity decline since the advent of tuning apps, they're still favored by many guitarists. Electronic tuners come in all shapes, sizes, and colors. Some of the most popular are of the clip-on variety, which fasten to your guitar's headstock. Unlike app tuners, which identify pitch via a built-in mic, clip-on tuners like the popular Snark brand pick up each string's pitch via vibrations from the headstock. The popularity of these tuners is due to accessibility and accuracy, as well as not having to use an instrument cable. Since clip-on tuners use vibration detection, environmental noise doesn't come between your guitar and the tuner, resulting in stable, precise tuning experiences. And some clip-on tuners even come with an external mic, allowing for sound-detection tuning, as well.

You can also find some multi-purpose electronic tuners that include several tuning modes (chromatic, guitar, ukulele, etc.), as well as a metronome. These tuners contain an instrument-cable input so you can connect your electric or acoustic-electric guitar for accurate tuning in loud environments. These tuners tend to be a little pricier than the clip-on models, but their multi-function capabilities might be appealing to you.

THE KEYBOARD METHOD

If you have a piano (or keyboard) handy, you can always tune your guitar's strings to the piano's corresponding keys.

Take a look at the diagram below. If you move 12 white keys to the left of middle C, you'll find the key that corresponds to the pitch of the low E string (string 6). Simultaneously pluck the string and sound the piano key until both pitches sound the same (i.e., are in tune). The piano's sustain pedal will come in handy here. From E, move up three white keys to find the key that matches the pitch of string 5, A. Sound both notes until the pitches match. Use the diagram to find the pitches for the remaining four strings: D, G, B, and E.

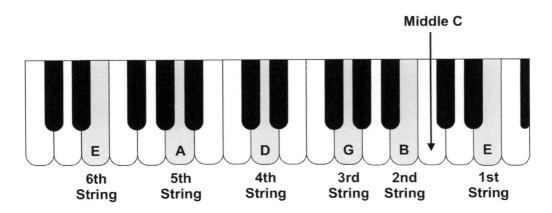

RELATIVE TUNING

Sometimes you'll find yourself stuck without a tuning source. Don't fret—you can use a method known as *relative tuning*. As long as your low E string is in tune—or at least close to its proper pitch—you can tune the other five strings so that the strings are in tune relative to one another.

Follow these steps:

1. Adjust your 6th (low E) string until you think it's in tune (for this purpose, close is good enough)

2. Fret the note at fret 5 of string 6, A, which is the same pitch as the open 5th string. Pluck this fretted note while also sounding the open 5th string. Adjust the pitch of string 5 until the two notes match.

3. Fret the note at fret 5 of string 5, D, which is the same pitch as the open 4th string. Pluck these two notes simultaneously, adjusting the pitch of string 4 until the two notes match.

4. Fret the note at fret 5 of string 4, G, which is the same pitch as the open 3rd string. Pluck these two notes simultaneously, adjusting the pitch of string 3 until the two notes match.

5. Fret the note at fret 4 of string 3, B, which is the same pitch as the open 2nd string. Pluck these two notes simultaneously, adjusting the pitch of string 2 until the two notes match.

6. Fret the note at fret 5 of string 2, E, which is the same pitch as the open 1st string. Pluck these two notes simultaneously, adjusting the pitch of string 1 until the two notes match.

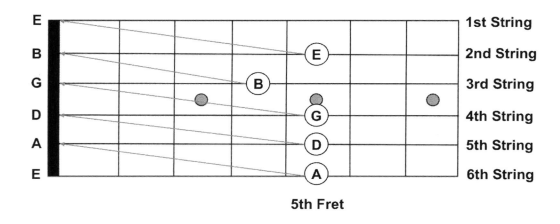

TUNING TO THE AUDIO

Now that you're acquainted with the aforementioned tuning methods, here's an easy one: download the tuning notes that accompany this book (all audio files are downloadable and can be found at *troynelsonmusic.com*). As you listen to each note, adjust the corresponding tuning peg until the string matches the recorded pitch. Once you've adjusted all six strings, your instrument should be in standard tuning: E–A–D–G–B–E (low to high).

OPEN E TUNING

As mentioned in the introduction, standard tuning is the tuning of choice for most guitarists. In fact, it's the default tuning for music written for guitar and most guitar instruction. When a piece of guitar music is to be played in anything other than standard tuning, a "tuning legend" will appear at the beginning of the piece to indicate which tuning should be employed. Usually, it will be a popular alternative such as Drop D, Open A, or DADGAD; other times, it may simply indicate a change in pitch of one or two strings.

Now that your guitar is in standard tuning, let's talk about how to get it into Open E. The reason I chose Open E tuning as the jumping-off point for beginners is because of its similarity to standard tuning. In fact, only three strings—the 5th, 4th, and 3rd—need to be adjusted to go from standard to Open E tuning. The other three strings—6th, 2nd, and 1st—remain the same.

Open E tuning (low to high: E–B–E–G#–B–E) gets its name from the fact that, when played together, the six strings form an E major (E–G#–B) triad (a three-note chord, although two of the pitches, E and B, are doubled here). While strings 6, 2, and 1 are already in tune and can remain unchanged, the other three strings (5, 4, and 3) need to be adjusted—but only slightly.

Let's start with string 5—the A string. We *could* lower it to G#, which is one of the notes in the E major chord, but instead we're going to raise it up to B. This relationship, E–B, helps facilitate some rhythm work that is common to guitar. Next, let's raise string 4, the D string, up to E, the root of the chord. Now we have *three* strings tuned to E (6th, 4th, and 1st). Be careful as you do this, however—you don't want to raise the pitch too high and risk breaking the string. Finally, our last adjustment will be to the 3rd string, G. All we need to do here is raise it up a bit, going from G to G# (in music, we call this distance a *half* step). Now your guitar should be in Open E tuning: E–B–E–G#–B–E (low to high). If you strum through all six strings, you should hear a nice, bright E major chord. If anything sounds amiss, check your tuning!

PROPER POSTURE

You can play the guitar two ways: sitting or standing. Neither approach is better than the other, and often context will determine which you use. For example, if you're playing in a band setting, then you'll most likely choose to stand (you might look rather silly sitting while your singer and bassist are standing). When you're in your bedroom practicing, you may choose to sit, especially if it's a long session. That said, standing while practicing is also a good habit to get into. In fact, some guitarists, while trying to increase stamina, will mimic their upcoming gigs by playing through their entire set list while standing.

SITTING

If you choose to sit, be sure to sit at the edge of your seat, with a relaxed posture. Set the guitar on the leg that's on the same side as your picking hand; for example, if you'll be strumming and picking the strings with your right hand, then set the guitar on your right leg. Conversely, if you'll be picking and strumming with your left hand, then place the guitar on your left leg. The guitar should rest on your thigh, near your torso, with the neck resting parallel to the floor.

STANDING

If you choose to stand, you will need a guitar strap, which fastens to strap buttons located on the upper bout and base of the guitar's body. Adjust the strap so that the guitar is positioned at the lower part of your torso, where your arms feel relaxed but not rigid. If you feel like you're having to reach too much with your arms to grip the neck and strum the strings, then you will likely need to raise the strap a bit. On the flip side, if you feel tension in your neck, shoulders, or arms, then you will need to loosen your strap. Strive for comfort.

PICKING & STRUMMING

Although fingerpicking will be covered throughout the book, the pick-hand technique we will focus on predominantly is flatpicking. *Flatpicking*, also known simply as "picking," involves plucking or strumming the strings with a flat, tear-shaped guitar pick. Most guitar picks are made from plastic or plastic-like materials and come in many sizes, colors, and thicknesses.

Choosing a pick that is best for you will take some time and is largely dependent on what style of music you play. If you find yourself mostly strumming folk songs, then a thin pick might be best because they tend to create a warmer sound than thick picks. Conversely, if you plan to play a lot of single-note lines (i.e., solos), then you might prefer a thicker pick. Experiment with as many types as you can; eventually, you will find one that speaks to you.

Hold the pick between the thumb and index finger of your pick hand. The more pick surface you leave exposed, the less control you will have over the pick. This approach is popular for strumming because it results in a warmer tone and you can be less precise with your strums.

If you plan to do a lot of single-note picking, you'll likely want to leave less pick surface exposed, gripping the pick near its tip. This gives you more control of the pick, resulting in more efficient upstrokes and downstrokes. In fact, in addition to gripping the pick near its tip, many guitarists will slant the pick semi-perpendicular to the strings to create less friction and, in turn, more speed.

CHORD DIAGRAMS & TAB

The music examples in this book will be presented in a couple of different formats: chord diagrams and tab. In this section, we're going to go over each format so you'll be able to quickly apply the music to your instrument as you go through the book. Let's start with chord diagrams.

CHORD DIAGRAMS

A *chord diagram*, or *chord frame*, is simply a graphical representation of a small section (usually four or five frets) of the guitar neck, or fretboard. Vertical lines represent the guitar's six strings, horizontal lines represent frets, and black dots indicate where your fingers should be placed. Although a bit counterintuitive, chord diagrams are presented as though you're looking at the neck while the guitar is held vertically in front of you rather than from a more natural horizontal position. Nevertheless, chord frames are a good way to quickly understand how a chord should be "voiced," or fingered.

A thick, black horizontal line at the top of the diagram indicates the guitar's nut (the plastic-like string-spacer at the end of the fretboard). When this is present, the chord typically incorporates one or more open strings, which are represented by hollow circles above the frame. Conversely, when an open string is not to be played, an "X" will appear above the frame.

When more than one note is fretted by the same finger, or "barred," a slur encompasses the notes. *Barre chords* get their name from this technique, which can range from just two strings to all six. If a chord is played higher up the neck, above the 4th of 5th fret, the nut is replaced by a thin horizontal line and the fret number is indicated next to the lowest fret (highest in the diagram). Sometimes—but not always—the chord's fingering is included at the bottom of the frame: 1 = index, 2 = middle, 3 = ring, 4 = pinky, and T = thumb.

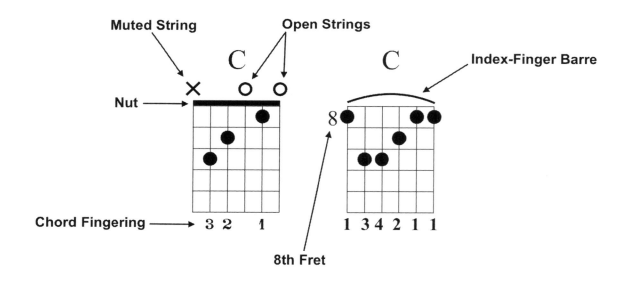

14

TAB

As a form of music notation, tab has been around for centuries. However, it has really exploded in popularity among guitar players the past few decades, particularly since the advent of the Internet. The reason for its popularity is the simple fact that it's so easy to learn.

A tab staff looks much like a standard treble or bass clef; however, if you look a little closer, you'll notice it contains *six* lines instead of five. Those six lines represent the six strings of the guitar, with the low E string positioned at the bottom, and the high E string at the top. Tab contains no key signature because there are no notes to deal with; instead, numbers are placed on the strings to represent the frets of the guitar neck. So, for example, if you see the number 3 on the 6th (low E) string, you would fret that string at fret 3. Or, if you see the number 0 stacked on the 3rd and 4th strings, you would strum those strings together, open (unfretted).

Sometimes you'll see tab accompanied by standard notation, and other times you'll see tab-only music (we'll be using the latter in this book). Tab-only music often includes rhythms (stems, flags, beams, rests, etc.), as well. Rhythm symbols in tab are the same as you'll find in standard notation, but the noteheads are replaced by fret numbers. Because we incorporate rhythm, the tab includes a time signature and requires a fundamental understanding of rhythm and rests, which we'll cover extensively throughout the book (unlike standard notation, we won't have to worry about key signatures, however).

The time signature is a pair of numbers that are stacked on top of each other and displayed on the staff at the beginning of a piece of music (immediately after the key signature in standard notation). The top number indicates how many beats comprise each *measure,* or *bar* (the space between the vertical *bar lines*), while the bottom number indicates which note is equivalent to one beat (2 = half note, 4 = quarter note, 8 = eighth note, etc.). All of the examples in this book are played in 4/4 time, meaning each measure contains four beats (upper number), and quarter notes are equivalent to one beat (bottom number).

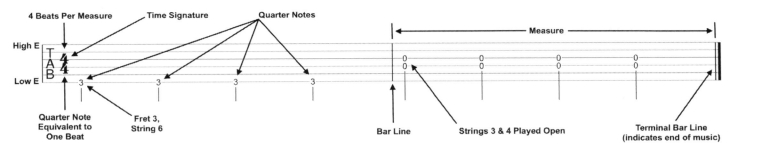

15

WEEK 1: OPEN E TUNING

If you haven't already, now's the time to tune your guitar to Open E: E–B–E–G#–B–E (low to high). As mentioned in the introduction, we're going to use this tuning throughout Week 1 to help you gain confidence in your playing before shifting to standard tuning in Week 2. (If you need a refresher, simply refer back to the Tuning Methods and Open E Tuning sections earlier in the book.)

DAY 1

BLUES SHUFFLE (1:30–1:15)

Blues shuffles are an excellent starting point for beginner guitarists because they sound great and they're relatively easy to play, particularly when played in Open E tuning like our exercise below. Set your metronome to approximately 50–60 beats per minute (BPM) and use a downstroke to strum (towards the floor) the bottom two strings open, letting them ring for four whole beats. If you recall from the introduction, quarter notes receive one beat in 4/4 time; here, however, we're dealing with *whole* notes, which receive *four* beats (whole notes = 4 beats, half notes = 2 beats, quarter notes = 1 beat, etc.).

When you get to measure 2, use your index finger to voice (fret) the note at fret 2 of string 5. Again, use a downward strum to pluck the two notes simultaneously, allowing them to ring out for all four beats. In measures 3–4, these two chords are repeated. The goal here is to target *just* the bottom two strings with our strums, avoiding the other four. However, if you happen to inadvertently include one or two of the other strings, it's not the end of the world because they belong to the same key (E major). That said, still try to limit your strums to just two strings.

STRUMMING (1:15–1:00)

This next example is an extension of the blues shuffle we just learned. Now, instead of limiting ourselves to two string, we're going to strum through all six of them. The first chord, E major, is pretty simple—it's all six strings played open. In measure 2, we move to an A chord (in this tuning, it's technically an Aadd9 chord) and, again, strum through all six strings. Voice this chord by placing your fret-hand's middle finger on fret 2 of string 5, and your index finger on fret 1 of string 3. The tricky part is preventing these fingers from unintentionally muting strings 4 and 2, so be sure to use the very tips of these fingers and add enough arch to get a full, clean six-string strum.

16

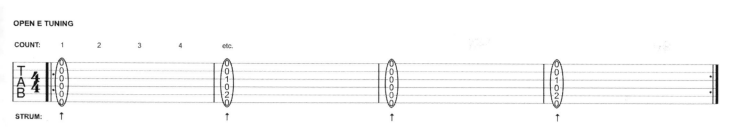

SINGLE-NOTE PICKING (1:00–0:45)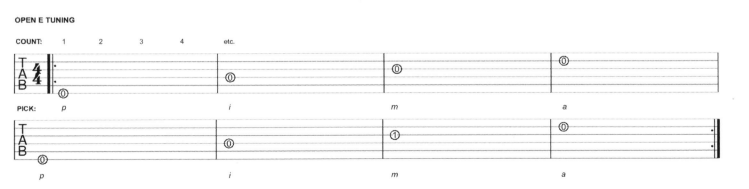

This exercise is the single-note version of our previous example. In measures 1–4, we're going to individually pluck the bottom four notes of our open E chord in a whole-note rhythm, allowing each note to ring out fully. In measures 5–8, we're going to give the same treatment to the A chord (it's the same chord as the one used in the Strumming example). Use downstrokes exclusively.

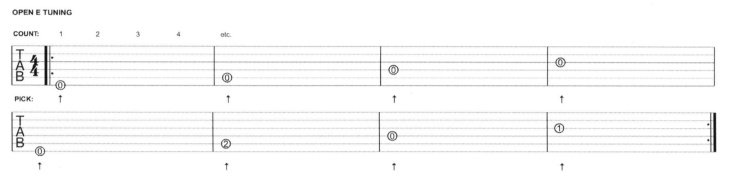

FINGERPICKING (0:45–0:30)

Our next exercise is going to be a bit more challenging. While it's similar to our previous example, the main difference is that now we're going to jettison our pick and, instead, use our fingers to pluck the strings. Like the previous example, allow each of the notes to ring out for four full beats, and use good finger arch to avoid unwanted string muting.

Measures 1–4 contain the E chord, and measures 5–8 are comprised of the A chord. For both chords, pluck string 6 with your thumb *(p)*, followed by your index *(i)*, middle *(m)*, and ring *(a)* fingers for strings 4, 3, and 2, respectively. Here's a tip: even though you won't be playing string 5, you should still voice the A chord fully; that is, place the middle finger of your fret hand on fret 2 of string 5 (in addition to your index finger on fret 1 of string 3).

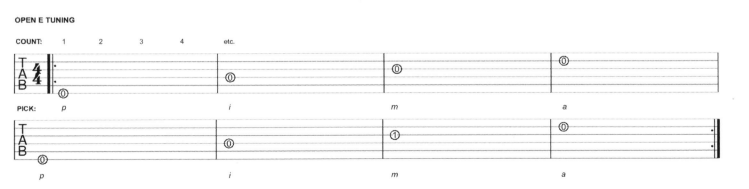

RESTS (0:30–0:15)

In this example, we're going to add periods of silence, or rest, to our chord strumming. Once again, we're going to use our trusty E and A chords. After strumming the E chord and holding it for a full four beats in measure 1, simultaneously (and gently) place your fret-hand fingers and the blade of your picking hand onto the strings to deaden them, allowing four beats of silence to occupy measure 2 (the symbol in measures 2, 4, 6 and 8 is a *whole rest* and, like a whole note, is equivalent to four beats). Repeat these steps for the A chord and whole rest in measures 3–4 (measures 5–8 are a second repetition of measures 1–4).

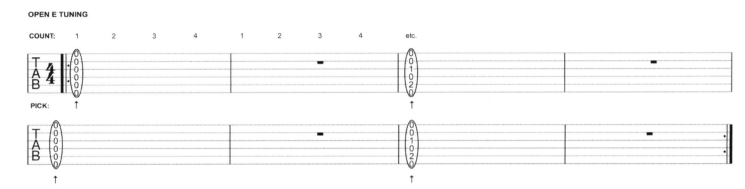

TECHNIQUE: NATURAL HARMONICS (0:15–0:00)

Natural harmonics are a great technique to get familiar with because they can add a nice texture to chord fills or perfectly punctuate a lead line in your solos, whether on acoustic or electric guitar. Playing harmonics requires an approach that's different from regularly fretted notes. Instead of placing the fingertip directly onto the string and pressing it to fretboard, lightly make contact with the string—without applying pressure and making contact with the neck—directly over the metal fret *wire* and then pluck it. The result should be a high-pitched bell-like tone (listen to the audio demo).

In the example below, gently lay your index finger across the wire at the 12th fret, making slight contact with the string without pressing it to the fretboard. Pluck each string with a downstroke and allow the harmonics to ring out for an entire measure (four beats). When you reach measure 5, reposition your fret hand over the 7th-fret wire and give each string the same treatment.

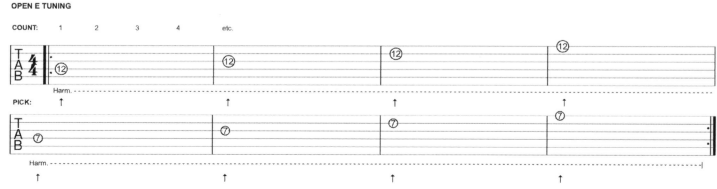

BLUES SHUFFLE (1:30–1:15)

The blues shuffle below is an extension of the one from yesterday. Here, the chord changes occur twice as fast, however, with half notes replacing the whole notes. Half notes receive two beats, so be sure to make the chord change on beat 3 of each measure, adding the index finger to fret 2 of string 5 for the new chord. This chord sequence is repeated in all four measures. Use downstrokes throughout, targeting just the lowest two strings with your pick.

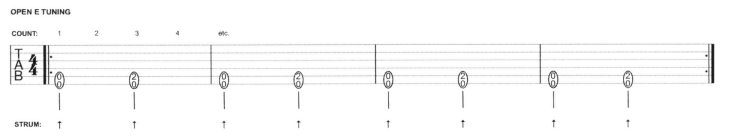

STRUMMING (1:15–1:00)

The E and A chords that were introduced in yesterday's strumming exercise are used here, as well; the only difference is that now we're going to play them in a half-note rhythm (like the previous example). Therefore, be sure to switch to the A chord on beat 3 of each measure, using the very tips of your fingers to voice this chord to prevent unwanted string muting (i.e., all six strings should ring out).

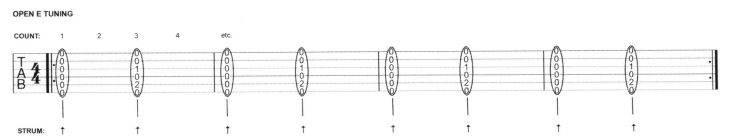

SINGLE-NOTE PICKING (1:00–0:45)

The chords used in this example should look familiar because they're the same E and A chords that we've been using for the past day and a half, and we're going to continue to use them throughout Week 1 so our primary focus can be on developing and improving pick-hand technique—without the challenges of learning and switching between new chords every day (in Week 2, our focus will shift to considerably more chord work).

As you can see, half notes are once again used exclusively. As you pluck the four notes that make up each chord, let them ring into one another rather than cutting them off. This is the effect we're going for, even though the tab notation doesn't reflect the longer note durations.

19

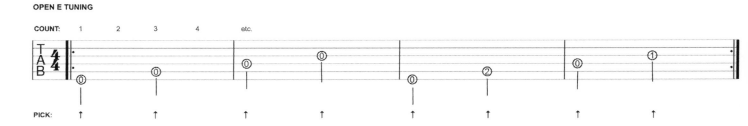

FINGERPICKING (0:45–0:30) 🔊

The fingerpicking pattern used in this next example is identical to the one used in yesterday's example—thumb (p) on string 6, index (i) on string 4, middle (m) on string 3, and ring (a) on string 2—as are the chord changes. The only difference is now the notes occur twice as fast because we're dealing with half notes rather than whole notes.

As before, when you switch to the A chord in measure 3, voice the chord fully, including the note at fret 2 of string 5. Even though that note is not played in this example, you may want to include it in the future. Voicing full chords while only plucking *some* of their notes is common practice on guitar, so it's best to get acclimated to it now.

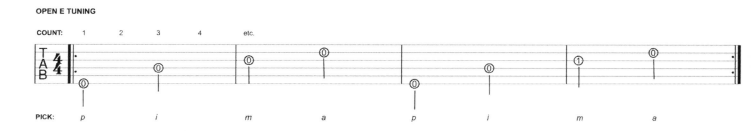

RESTS (0:30–0:15) 🔊

Next up is the half rest. If you haven't figured it out already, a *half rest* indicates two beats of silence in music written in 4/4 time, the same duration as half notes. If you look at the counting prompt above the tab staff below, you'll notice that, in each measure, the chord receives two beats (beats 1 and 2) and the half rest receives two beats (beats 3 and 4). This chord/rest dichotomy is repeated in each of the four measures. As mentioned yesterday, after strumming the chord and holding it for two beats, simultaneously rest your fret-hand fingers and the blade of your pick hand on the strings to deaden them, keeping them silent until it's time to strum the next chord.

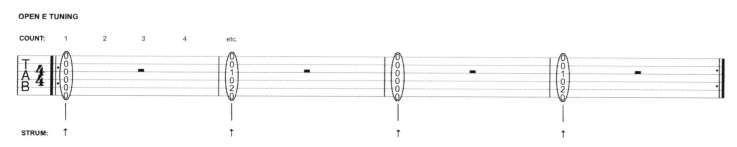

TECHNIQUE: STRING BENDING (0:15–0:00)

String bending is a technique that enables guitarists to raise the pitch of a string without having to move to a new fret. It's a very emotive technique because it brings out the microtonal pitches that exist between the typical half- and whole-step intervals that comprise Western music, giving guitar lines a vocal-like quality.

Most bends are of the half- or whole-step variety (the distance of one and two frets, respectively), but we're going to focus on another popular type, quarter-step bends, which are much easier to execute. The example below is a bluesy bass-string riff that involves bending strings 4–6 at the 3rd fret, each a quarter step. Each bend is immediately followed by an open string, which allows enough time to reposition the fret hand for the subsequent bend.

Use your fret-hand index finger to perform each bend, slowly pulling the string downward (toward the floor) in a smooth motion over the course of two beats (a half note) to raise the string's pitch ever so slightly. Before you attempt this exercise, be sure to give the audio demo a listen so you can hear the bends in action.

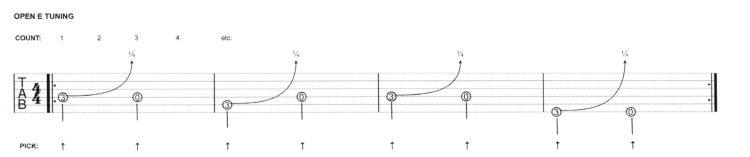

BLUES SHUFFLE (1:30–1:15)

Rhythmically, we've worked extensively with whole and half notes, and now it's time to introduce the next rhythmic subdivision: quarter notes. As previously mentioned, *quarter notes* are equivalent to one beat in 4/4 time. So, when performing the shuffle below, the chords must be strummed on *every* click of your metronome—twice as frequently as the half notes in yesterday's example. Note that, even though we're strumming on every beat, the chord change doesn't occur until beat 3 in each measure. In other words, we'll strum the open strings twice, then add our index finger to fret 2 of string 5, strumming this chord twice, as well.

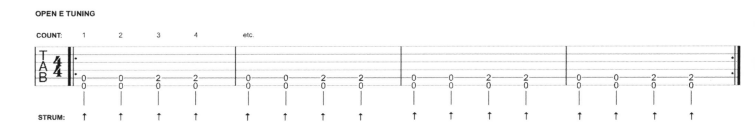

STRUMMING (1:15–1:00)

Here's the strumming version of the blues shuffle that we just worked on. Again, strum the strings in a quarter-note rhythm (every beat), changing chords at the midpoint (beat 3) of each measure. Use downstrokes throughout.

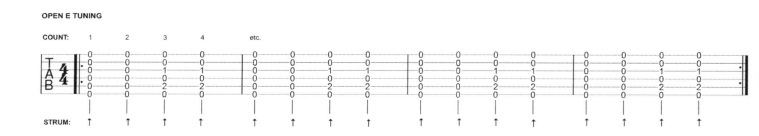

SINGLE-NOTE PICKING (1:00–0:45)

Now we're going to arpeggiate (an *arpeggio* is the notes of a chord played individually) in a quarter-note rhythm the chords we just strummed. Hopefully, you've got a good handle on the A chord (measures 2 and 4) by now because the notes move at a pretty good clip. If you remember to keep your middle and ring fingers arched, using just the very tips, you should be good to go.

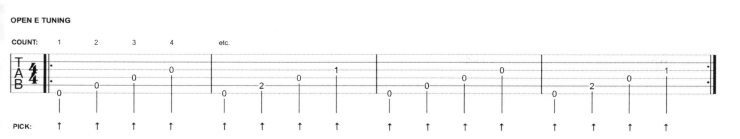

FINGERPICKING (0:45–0:30) 🔊

This exercise is the quarter-note version of yesterday's fingerpicking example. Although the notes occur at a faster pace, the fingerpicking pattern remains the same: *p–i–m–a* (thumb–index–middle–ring). As before, we'll be skipping over string 5, so be sure to apply each finger to the correct string. Once there, you can keep the fingers in place throughout the exercise.

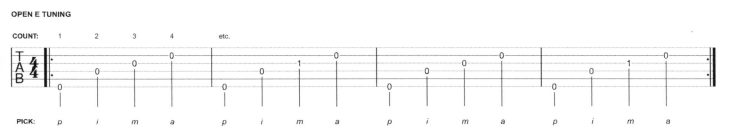

RESTS (0:30–0:15) 🔊

The biggest challenge here is muting the rests, especially at this quarter-note pace. For best results, implement the same muting technique that we used on Days 1 and 2—that is, a combination of the fret and pick hands—and use the brief pause (quarter-note rest) on beat 2 to begin positioning your middle and index fingers for the A chord that appears on beat 3 of each measure. Once again, use downstrokes throughout.

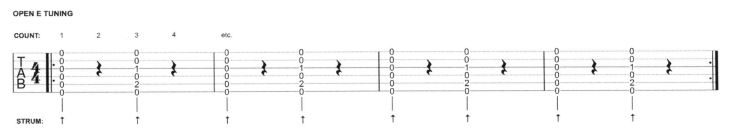

TECHNIQUE: HAMMER-ON (0:15–0:00)

A *hammer-on* is a technique that is used in both rhythm and lead guitar playing and involves plucking a fretted (or open) string and then sounding the subsequent note by "hammering" onto the string with another fret-hand finger—without re-striking the string with your pick.

In the exercise below, our familiar E and A chords each occupy a full measure. At the end of measure 2, however, the middle finger of the fret hand performs a hammer-on that moves from the open 5th string to the 2nd fret. When executing this hammer-on, leave your index finger in place (fret 1, string 3) so the upper portion of the chord can ring through the entire measure.

The second hammer-on (measure 4), involves hammering the index finger from the open 3rd string to the 1st fret. Similar to the previous hammer-on, leave the middle finger in place so the lower portion of the chord can ring through the entire measure

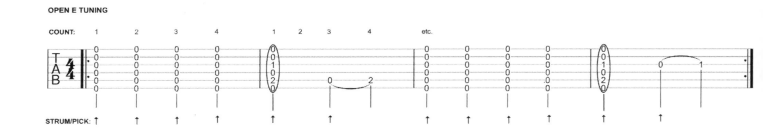

BLUES SHUFFLE (1:30–1:15)

Today, we're going to continue rhythmic subdividing, this time splitting our quarter notes into eighth notes. The strong beats (downbeats) are still counted as normal ("1, 2, 3, 4," etc.), but the weak beats (upbeats) are counted with an ampersand (&), giving us the following: "1 & 2 & 3 & 4 &," etc. Keep this counting prompt running in your head, or even say it out loud, while you strum *every* eighth-note subdivision with a downstroke. In addition to our new rhythm, the chords change at a more rapid pace compared to previous days, alternating every beat rather than every other beat.

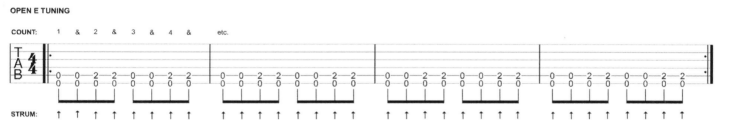

STRUMMING (1:15–1:00)

We're going to pick up the pace in this strumming exercise, as well. Comprised entirely of eighth notes, the figure switches between E and A chords every two beats. If you look at the strumming prompt below the tab staff, you'll notice that we're going to alternate downstrokes and upstrokes with each eighth note. This technique has a different feel to it than using downstrokes exclusively, so don't get discouraged if it takes a little extra time to get comfortable with it.

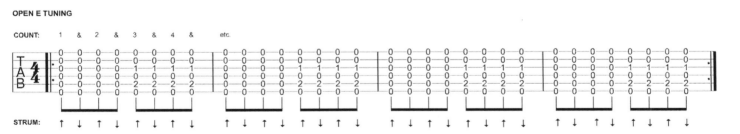

SINGLE-NOTE PICKING (1:00–0:45)

The picking exercise below features a steady stream of eighth notes. The notes themselves are identical to the ones from yesterday's picking exercise, but now the chord's change twice as fast due to the eighth-note rhythm. As you arpeggiate the chords exclusively with downstrokes, let each note ring out fully. And don't forget to use the counting prompt ("1 & 2 & 3 & 4 &," etc.), reciting it either mentally or verbally as you go along.

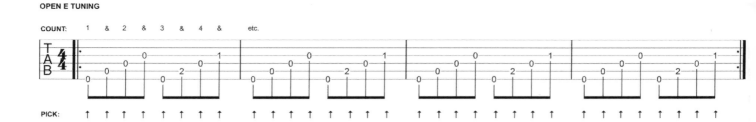

FINGERPICKING (0:45–0:30)

This exercise is a continuation of the fingerpicking we've covered over the first few days. In fact, the chords, picking pattern (*p–i–m–a*), and string choices are all the same, only now we're playing the figure in an eighth-note rhythm (notice a trend?). As before, be sure to include your middle finger (on fret 2, string 5) when voicing the A chord, even though it's not plucked. This is a good habit to get into.

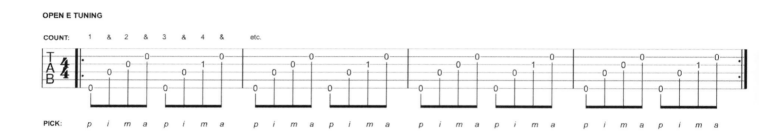

RESTS (0:30–0:15)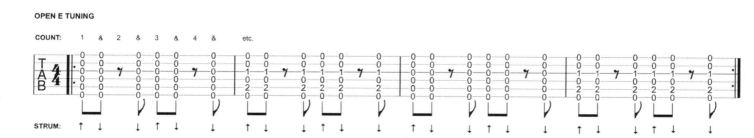

This exercise gives us our first taste of *syncopation*, the practice of stressing weak beats. Syncopation can range from subtle to extreme. Our exercise falls somewhere in between, with eighth-note rests falling on beats 2 and 4 to set up chord strums on the upbeats.

Notice that alternate strumming is employed throughout. However, due to the rests, downstrokes are not necessary on beats 2 and 4 of each measure. Instead, you'll want to employ the muting technique that we used for rests in previous exercises. Make sure that, when you bring the blade of your strumming hand down onto the strings to mute, you position the pick near the treble (higher) strings so it's in position for the upstroke that occurs immediately after the rest.

TECHNIQUE: PULL-OFF (0:15–0:00)

Modeled after the hammer-on exercise from yesterday, this example forgoes the aforementioned hammer-ons in favor of a pair of 3rd-string pull-offs. A *pull-off* is essentially the opposite of a hammer-on. Instead of moving up in pitch, a pull-off involves sounding a lower pitch by "pulling off" from one finger to another (or an open string) on the same string. In our case, we're going to pull off with our index finger from fret 1 to the open 3rd string.

One other thing worth noting is the reverse arpeggiation that occurs just before the pull-off. These notes are simply the top three notes of the A chord (so keep it voiced!), with the 3rd-fret note, A, being pulled off to the open pitch, G#, thereby facilitating the return of the E chord.

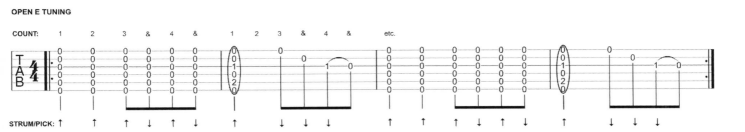

BLUES SHUFFLE (1:30–1:15)

We're going to spice up today's blues shuffle by adding an extra note, D, which is located at fret 3 of string 5 and should be fretted with the middle finger (the 2nd-fret note, C#, is fretted with the index finger). You'll be tempted to shift your index finger back and forth between fret 2 and fret 3, but do your best to keep your fingers in place, with your index assigned to fret 2 and your middle assigned to fret 3.

The rhythm is the same as yesterday's shuffle (i.e., strict eighth notes), but now, instead of strumming open strings on beat 3 of each measure, we're going to introduce our new note, D, to the festivities. Other than that, everything else is exactly the same.

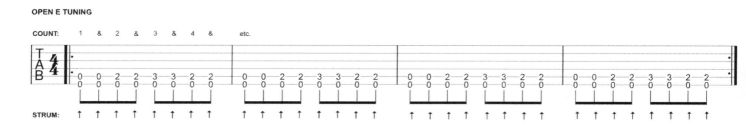

STRUMMING (1:15–1:00)

Like our previous example, this exercise also introduces a new element—in this case, a B major chord (in Open E tuning, it's technically a Badd4 chord). The voicing for this chord is identical to the A chord we've been using—including the open 1st, 2nd, 4th, and 6th string—only it's voiced two frets higher. Consequently, moving from A to B (or vice versa) is a snap.

When transitioning between the A and B chords, be sure to maintain your alternate (down–up–down–up) strumming because a momentary pause will result in an unintended rest. Here's a tip: When changing between these two chords, simply slide your middle and index fingers up (or down) the strings rather than lifting your fingers from the fretboard and having to reset them for the next chord.

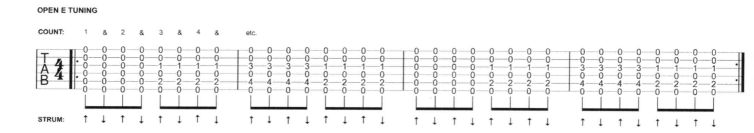

SINGLE-NOTE PICKING (1:00–0:45)

Now, we're going to take our new E–A–B–A progression and pick the notes individually while main-taining our familiar eighth-note rhythm. Use downstrokes throughout, letting the notes of each chord ring out fully. And don't forget: transition between the A and B chords by sliding up and down the strings rather than lifting your fret hand from the fretboard and having to reapply it.

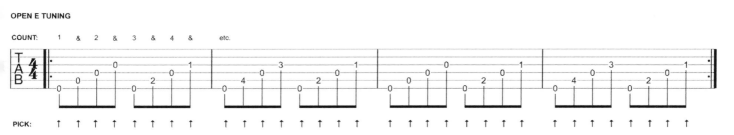

FINGERPICKING (0:45–0:30)

By now, you should be getting at least somewhat comfortable with the *p–i–m–a* picking pattern. If not, well, you're in luck because we're going to practice it one more time. In the example below, the pattern is applied to our E–A–B–A progression. As before, be sure to voice the A and B chords fully (even though we're skipping over the fretted pitches on string 5), letting the notes ring to their fullest potential.

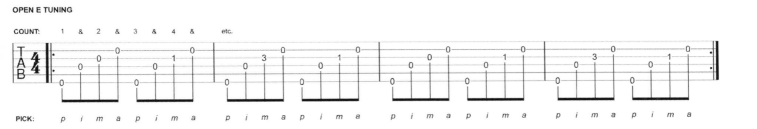

RESTS (0:30–0:15)

In this next example, we're going to combine quarter and eighth notes and rests to create a syncopat-ed exercise not unlike the one from yesterday. Here, however, there is complete silence (i.e., a quar-ter-note rest) on beat 2 of each measure, and the syncopation occurs on the "and" (upbeat) of beat 3 rather than on beats 2 and 4.

The tricky part of this example is to not rush the syncopated strum on the "and' of beat 3, which is easy to do following one-and-a-half beats of rest. This is where counting comes in really handy. Also, listening to and playing along with the audio demo will help you get it just right.

TECHNIQUE: SLIDE (0:15–0:00) 🔊

We've discussed slides in previous exercises, but now you get an opportunity to see them notated in the tab. In the example below, we're going to slide between the A and B chords on beat 1 of each measure. The main difference between this example and previous ones is that we want these slides to be more deliberate; that is, we want the slides to stand out among the chord strumming. Additionally, these are *legato* slides, meaning we don't pick/strum the strings once the slides reach their destination (indicated by the two slurs), unlike our previous examples. Be careful here, as it's easy to rush these types of slides. We want the initial attack and slide to occur in time with the eighth-note rhythm.

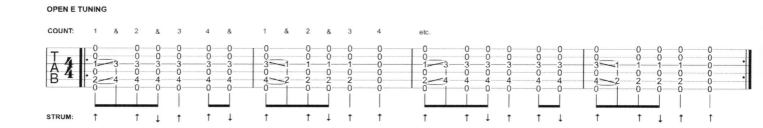

BLUES SHUFFLE (1:30–1:15)

After five days of sticking to the first few frets, today's shuffle ventures into uncharted territory, moving up to fret 5 to transpose the riff to another key. In music, the term *transpose* means to move a piece of music to a higher or lower collection of pitches, or key. In our case, we play the riff in its original key, E, in measures 1–2, and then transpose the riff to the key of A in measures 3–4 by playing it at the 5th fret. This chord movement, I to IV ("one to four"), is a key component of blues harmony.

While the first half of this riff should be relatively easy by now, the second half will take some time getting used to. To perform this riff, barre strings 5–6 at the 5th fret with the area above the first knuckle of your index finger, just below the fingertip. Then, on beats 2 and 4, fret string 5 at the 7th fret with your ring finger (the pinky will work, too, although the ring finger is recommended) while keeping the index finger in position at the 5th fret. Keeping the two-finger barre in place at fret 5 is most efficient and will prevent any unintended pauses.

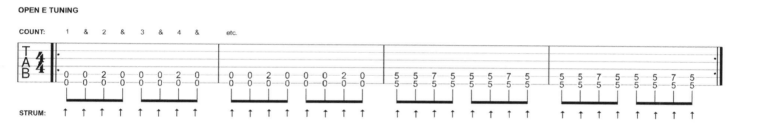

STRUMMING (1:15–1:00)

Following two days of mostly eighth-note rhythms, today we're going to explore the next logical sub-division: 16th notes. In 4/4 time, 16th notes divide each beat into four equal parts, counted: "1 e & a, 2 e & a, 3 e & a, 4 e & a," etc. In the exercise below, our E, A, and B chords are strummed in a strict 16th-note rhythm. Like our previous eighth-note examples, alternate strumming is used throughout, only the repetitions are twice as fast (when played at the same tempo) now. Take this one really slow at first, somewhere in the neighborhood of 40 BPM.

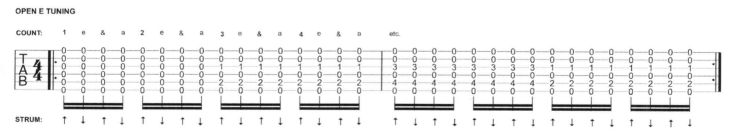

SINGLE-NOTE PICKING (1:00–0:45)

We briefly touched on reverse arpeggiation in the Technique section on Day 4, but today we're going to give this technique a good workout. In the exercise below, the open E chord occupies two beats. On beat 1, the chord is ascended from string 6 to string 3. Then, on beat 2, the direction is reversed and the chord is descended from string 2 to string 5. This pattern is then repeated for each new chord.

Pay attention to the picking prompt below the tab staff. You'll be tempted to use a downstroke at the top of beat 2, but an upstroke is a better choice because it enables you to use upstrokes exclusively on this beat. Like the previous exercise, start very slowly, gradually increasing your tempo as you feel more comfortable and make fewer mistakes.

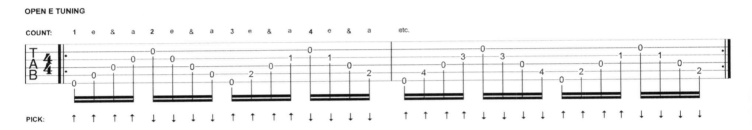

FINGERPICKING (0:45–0:30)

Following several days of straight *p–i–m–a* fingerpicking, it's time to switch things up a bit. In the exercise below, we'll be working on a couple of techniques, *reverse arpeggios* and *alternating-thumb picking.*

Notice that, as the arpeggiations ascend and descend the E, A, and B chords, the thumb alternates between string 6 (beats 1 and 3) and string 5 (beats 2 and 4). Fortunately, the index *(i)*, middle *(m)*, and ring *(a)* fingers never deviate from strings 4, 3, and 2, respectively, so our full attention can be focused on nailing the thumb's movement.

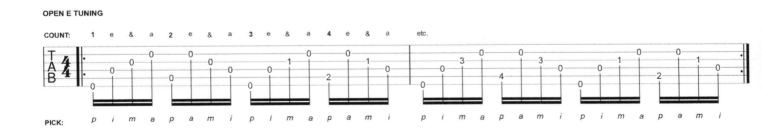

RESTS (0:30–0:15)

We're going to stick with our 16th-note theme here and introduce the 16th-note rest, which has the same rhythmic value as a 16th note. In the exercise below, 16th-note rests are placed on the "and" (upbeat) of each beat to break up what would otherwise be a steady stream of 16th notes. The result is some pretty aggressive syncopation, courtesy of the 16th-note chord strums that fall on the very last 16th-note subdivision (counted as "a") of each beat.

Be sure to use the 16th-note counting ("1-e-&-a, 2-e-&-a," etc.) throughout, as well as the muting technique that we used for the syncopated eighth-note strumming back on Day 4. That is, as you bring your strumming hand down onto the strings (in concert with the fret hand) to do the muting, make sure to position the pick as close to the treble strings as possible to set it up for the forthcoming upstroke. Once you have the pattern down for the first chord, E, the other chords should come much easier because they use the same pattern.

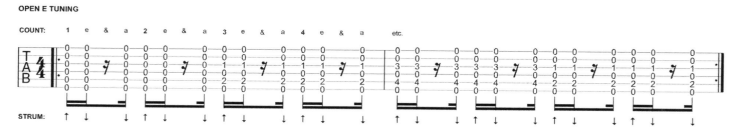

TECHNIQUE: MUTED STRUMMING (0:15–0:00)

Muted strumming is a technique that is used in just about every style of music, from folk and rock to reggae and funk. The technique is similar to the one we've been using for rests, but instead of striving for silence, we're going to actually strum the muted strings to produce a percussive effect.

As you strum all six strings in a 16th-note rhythm, offset the chords (beats 1 and 3) with muted strums (beats 2 and 4). Since the pick hand is busy with the strumming, we're going to use the fret hand exclusively for the muting. The key to this technique is keeping the strum momentum going in the pick hand, swiftly moving the fret hand between the chord voicings and the muting, which can be executed by gently laying all four fingers across all six strings, being careful not to push the strings all the way down to the fretboard.

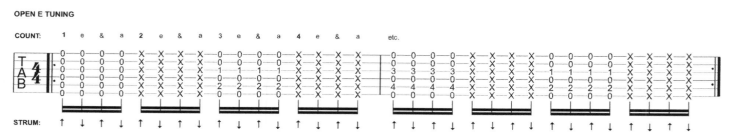

BLUES SHUFFLE (1:30–1:15)

The exercise below is a hybrid of the blues shuffles from Days 5 and 6. Like yesterday's example, this one moves up to fret 5 in measure 3 to reproduce in the key of A the E major riff that's introduced in measure 1–2. The main difference here, however, is that we have more movement along string 5 (which is similar to Day 5's shuffle). As you barre the lowest two strings at fret 5 with your index finger, use your ring finger to reach up and grab the note at fret 7, followed by your pinky for the note at fret 8. Alternate between these three fingers as you perform the figure in measures 3–4.

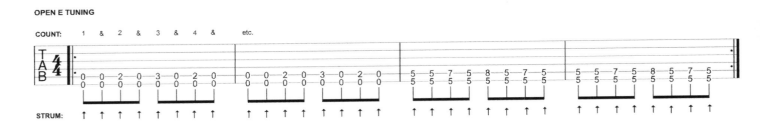

STRUMMING (1:15–1:00)

Now that we've got whole, half, quarter, eighth, and 16th notes under our belts, it's time to mix them up a bit. The music figure below combines quarter notes, eight notes, and 16th notes for a fairly straight-ahead strumming exercise. This is the first time we've encountered the eighth-and-two-16ths grouping (beats 2 and 4), so use the counting prompt and audio demonstration for help. Also, be sure to follow the picking instructions located below the tab staff. Although you might be inclined to use an upstroke on the first 16th note of the groupings, the more efficient choice is a *down*-up strum combo for the 16th-note pairs, which will set up your pick hand for a downstroke on the next downbeat.

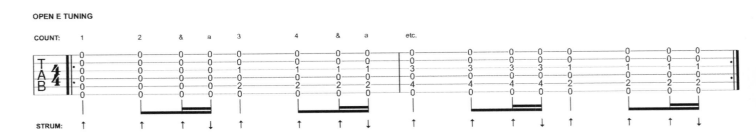

SINGLE-NOTE PICKING (1:00–0:45)

Rhythmically, this exercise is identical to the previous one, so counting it should be familiar. The biggest challenges here are the pair of string skips required: when ascending from string 5 to string 3, and when descending from string 4 to string 6. To pick this exercise, start with back-to-back downstrokes, followed by a pair of upstrokes. Then repeat this pattern for each new chord.

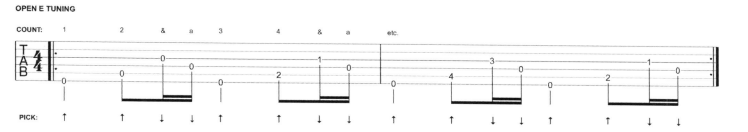

FINGERPICKING (0:45–0:30)

This exercise is identical to the single-note example we just worked on, only now we're going to pluck the strings with our fingers. The thumb leads things off and is followed by a middle-index combo for the 16th notes. As before, keep your index (i), middle (m), and ring (a) fingers planted on strings 4, 3, and 2, respectively, using your thumb to alternate between strings 6 and 5.

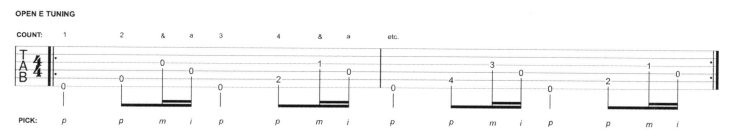

RESTS (0:30–0:15)

Now it's time to introduce a couple of important rhythmic devices used in music: the *dot* and the *tie*. A *dot* increases the duration of the note it accompanies by one half of the note's original rhythmic value. For example, in the exercise below, the quarter note on beat 1 of each measure is accompanied by a dot, which increases the note's value from one beat to one-and-a-half beats.

Ties function in much the same way as dots. A *tie* is a curved line that connects two notes of the same pitch and indicates that the notes are to be played as one, with the duration equal to the sum of the individual notes' rhythmic value. In the example below, eighth notes (half a beat) are tied to quarter notes (one beat); therefore, these chords should be held for a total of one-and-a-half beats (incidentally, the same value as the dotted quarter notes).

Notes are not the only thing that can be accompanied by dots; rests can, too. At the end of measure 2, a dotted-eighth-note rest precedes a 16th note. Since an eight note is equivalent to half a beat, the dot has the rhythmic value of a *quarter* beat. Therefore, the duration of a dotted-eighth-note rest—as well as a dotted eighth *note*—is three quarters of a beat. Be sure to count this beat slowly at first because it's easy to rush the 16th-note chord strum, coming in on the "and" rather than the "a."

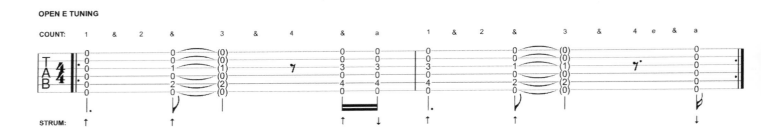

TECHNIQUE: PALM MUTING (0:15–0:00)

The rhythm used in this example should look familiar because it's the same one we've used on several occasions today. But now we're going to add in one of guitar's most ubiquitous techniques, *palm muting*.

Following each quarter-note chord strum (beats 1 and 3), we're going to palm-mute the low E string in the eighth-and-two-16ths rhythm (known as a "gallop") that we worked on earlier. To execute the palm mutes, gently place the blade of your pick hand on string 6, leaving it in place while you pick the notes. The result should be a muted, punchy attack (listen to the audio demo to hear how the palm mutes should sound). Also, don't overlook the suggested picking for the gallops: down–*down*–up. The back-to-back downstrokes will set you up for a downstroke on the subsequent downbeat (beats 1 and 3).

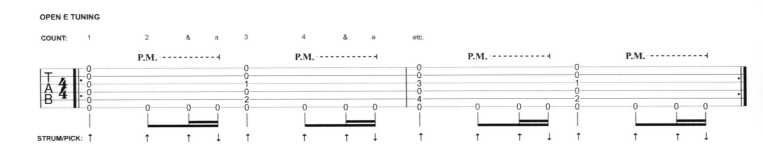

WEEK 2: STANDARD TUNING

Congratulations! You've made it through Week 1 and, hopefully, are ready to tackle Week 2. By now, you should be starting to feel more confident in your strumming and single-note picking, as well as getting acclimated to making chord changes with your fret hand. After focusing primarily on the pick hand in Week 1, the next seven days are going to give your fret hand a real workout as you learn to voice an abundance of common guitar chords. But, first, it's time to change tunings.

To switch from Open E (E–B–E–G#–B–E, low to high) to standard tuning (E–A–D–G–B–E, low to high), which we'll use throughout Week 2, we'll need to make three simple changes:

1.   Tune the 5th string down one whole step, from B to A
2.   Tune the 4th string down one whole step, from E to D
3.   Tune the 3rd string down one *half* step, from G# to G

(If you need a refresher on tuning, simply refer back to the Tuning Methods section in the book's introduction.)

DAY 8

BLUES SHUFFLE (1:30–1:15)

Now that we're in *standard tuning*, we're going to review some of the exercises that we learned in Open E tuning. While Open E is a great tuning to explore and for playing certain types of music, standard tuning is the, well… gold standard in guitar playing.

The example below is the standard-tuned version of the very first example that we worked on. The only difference is that now the notes along string 5 are played at frets 2 and 4 instead of open and fret 2. Use your index finger in bars 1 and 3, and your ring finger in bars 2 and 4, allowing the low E string to ring freely throughout.

STRUMMING (1:15–1:00)

Last week, we learned E, A, and B chords relative to Open E tuning. Today, we're going to focus on the first two, E and A, and how to voice them in *standard* tuning. The two shapes presented here are common open chords (*open chords* are chords played near the nut, or "open position," and contain open strings). Notice that the E chord shape here is similar to the A chord shape in Open E tuning; therefore, the amount of time spent getting acclimated to this chord should be minimal.

The A chord, however, will take a little more effort. The fingering suggested here involves placing our index, middle, and ring fingers on strings 4, 3, and 2, respectively—all on the same fret (fret 2). There is an alternative to this fingering, however, which involves using our index finger to barre these three strings. Although string 1 is played open in the diagram shown below, with the index-finger-barre voicing, we would simply mute that string with the underside of our index finger, or just not include that string when we strum.

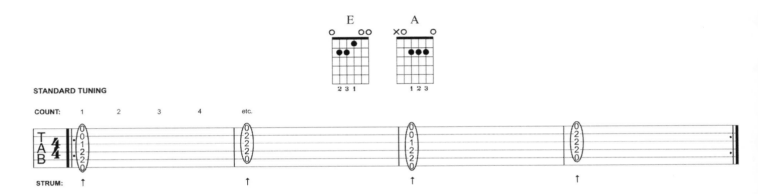

SINGLE-NOTE PICKING (1:00–0:45)

In this exercise, we're going to continue to focus on the standard-tuned open E and A chords that we just learned. Instead of strumming them, however, we're going to arpeggiate them in a slow, whole-note rhythm, which should give us enough time to "make the changes." Here's a tip: As you let the last note of the E chord ring out (measure 4), start mentally preparing yourself to switch to the A chord at the top of measure 5. And, since the first note of the A chord is played open, you'll have a little extra time to get your fingers into place.

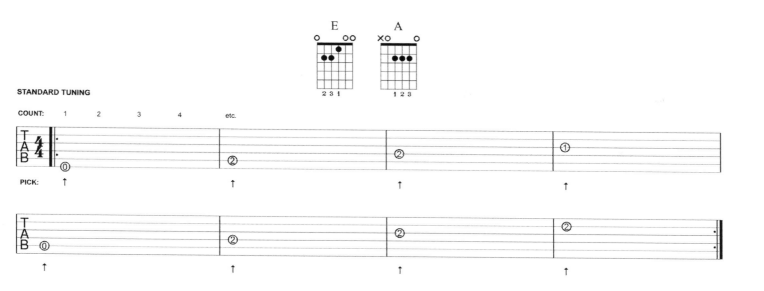

FINGERPICKING (0:45–0:30)

Our familiar *p–i–m–a* fingerpicking pattern makes a return for this next example. Throughout the exercise, keep your index *(i)*, middle *(m)*, and ring *(a)* fingers planted on strings 4, 3, and 2, respectively, while your thumb moves between strings 6 and 5 as the chords change.

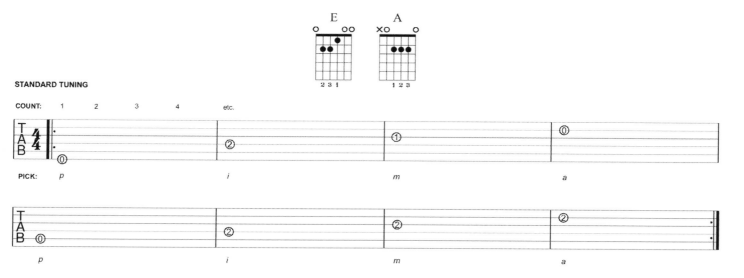

CHORD PROGRESSION (0:30–0:15)

Now it's time to string together a few chords to create a progression. A *chord progression* is a series of chords used as the harmonic foundation of a music composition, or song, and is the music component upon which melodies are built.

In the exercise below, C, Am, Dm, and G chords are played sequentially and in a whole-note rhythm. All of the chords are "diatonic" to the key of C major, meaning they all belong to the same chord "family," with C being the "parent" chord.

When moving from C to Am, keep your index and middle fingers affixed to the strings, moving only your ring finger, which is relocated from fret 3, string 5 to fret 2, string 3. As you hold out each chord, mentally prepare yourself for the impending change; that is, visualize where your fingers will move when you switch from one chord to the other.

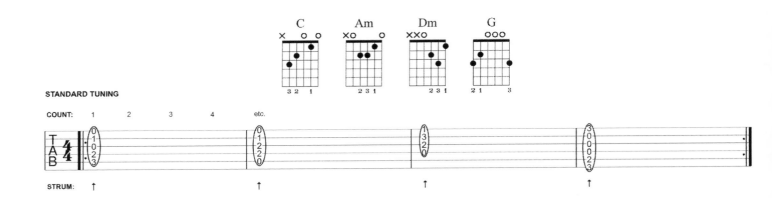

SCALE (0:15–0:00)

Enough about chords for now; let's turn our attention to another important component of music, scales. When we create melodies, we use scales as the source for our pitches. For example, if we were to write a melody over the top of the chord progression we just learned, C–Am–Dm–G, we would borrow notes from the C major scale because the chords are diatonic (in the key of) C major. So, let's start with that scale.

Below is a common pattern for the C major scale (C–D–E–F–G–A–B). Since no open strings are involved, we can move this pattern up or down the fretboard to play it in other keys. To do so, we just need to shift the scale's root notes (white dots in the fretboard diagram) to the root of the new key.

For now, were just going to practice the scale in ascending fashion, moving from the 6th-string root to the 1st-string root. Use alternate (down–up–down–up) picking throughout, and pay attention to the fingering suggestions indicated below the staff (1 = index, 2 = middle, 3 = ring, 4 = pinky).

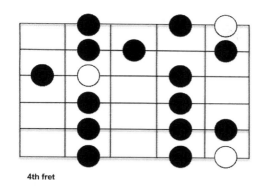

4th fret

STANDARD TUNING

COUNT: 1   2   3   4   etc.

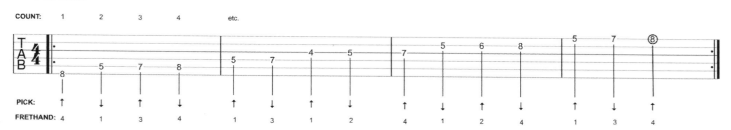

PICK: ↑   ↓   ↑   ↓   ↑   ↓   ↑   ↓   ↑   ↓   ↑   ↓   ↑   ↓   ↑

FRETHAND: 4   1   3   4   1   3   1   2   4   1   2   4   1   3   4

BLUES SHUFFLE (1:30–1:15)

Today, we're going to start by modifying yesterday's blues shuffle, speeding it up by replacing whole notes with half notes (the same rhythmic subdividing we did last week). Now the index-to-ring alternations occur in *every* measure rather than across two bars. Use downstrokes throughout—and don't forget to count!

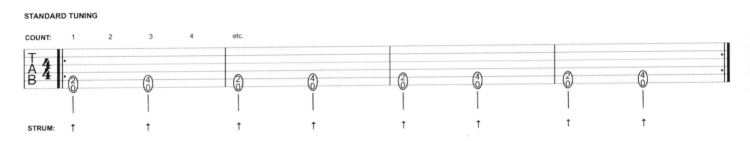

STRUMMING (1:15–1:00)

Like our previous example, we're going to speed up the chord changes in this exercise by replacing whole notes with half notes. Likewise, we're going to use the same E and A chords, so the familiarity should help flatten out the learning curve a bit. Remember: If the A chord voicing shown here is too difficult, don't hesitate to use an index-finger barre. Just don't forget to mute the 1st string.

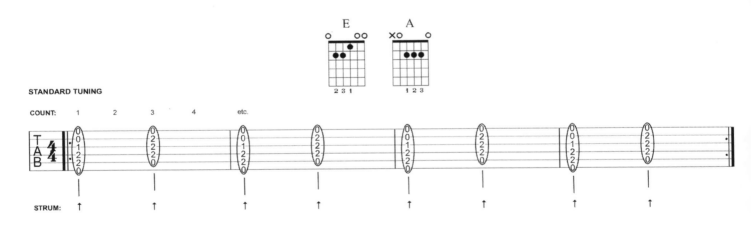

SINGLE-NOTE PICKING (1:00–0:45)

Now let's arpeggiate our E and A chords in a half-note rhythm. Like before, use the open 5th string (root of the A chord) at the top of measure 3 to your advantage. As the string rings open, use that extra time to get your index, middle, and ring fingers in place for the remainder of the arpeggiation (this strategy works well when the E chord comes around again, too).

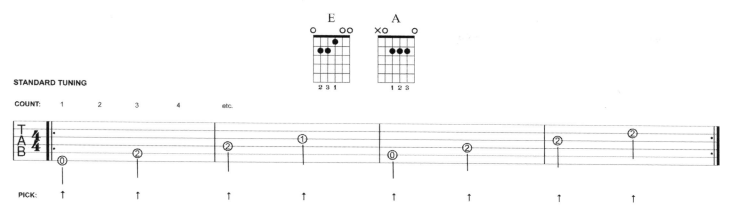

FINGERPICKING (0:45–0:30)

Here's the fingerpicking version of the previous exercise. We're utilizing the *p–i–m–a* pattern once again, which means we'll need to keep the index *(i)*, middle *(m)*, and ring (a) fingers paired with strings 4, 3, and 2, respectively, while the thumb moves between strings 6 and 5 as the chords change.

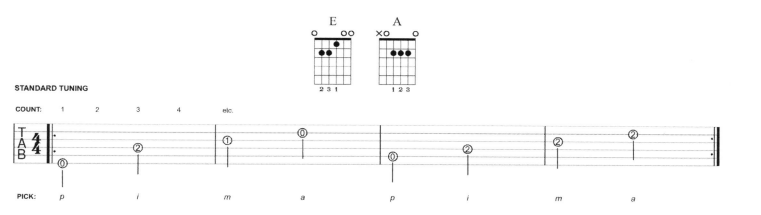

CHORD PROGRESSION (0:30–0:15)

This progression features two new chords, Em and D. While yesterday's progression was firmly rooted in C major, this group of chords, played in this order, implies E *minor*. While the Em chord is relatively easy to voice, the D chord might give you a bit of trouble, particularly the middle finger (string 1). If this is the case, a good workaround is to focus on getting your index and ring fingers in place on strings 3 and 2, respectively, and strumming just strings 4–2 (muting string 1). Eventually, you'll want to include string 1 in your D chord, but this approach should help in the interim.

43

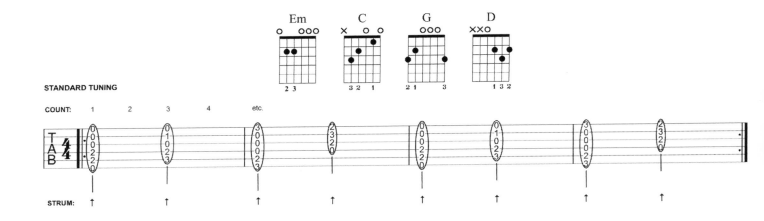

SCALE (0:15–0:00)

This pattern is the descending version of the C major scale that we learned yesterday. Playing it this way might feel a bit awkward at first because, when it comes to scales, descending is always more difficult than ascending, for some reason. Nevertheless, use the same approach as before: use alternate picking, change notes in a quarter-note rhythm, and follow the fingering suggestions notated below the staff.

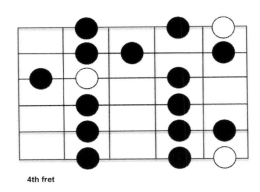

4th fret

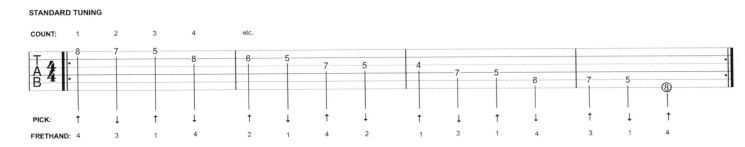

BLUES SHUFFLE (1:30–1:15)

In this shuffle, we're going to continue picking up the pace, this time replacing half notes with quarter notes. Ideally, you'd like to keep your index finger planted on fret 2 while you reach up to fret 4 with the ringer finger, but if this stretch is uncomfortable, feel free to alleviate some of the tension by lifting the index from the fretboard ever so slightly, then replanting it when it's time to fret it again.

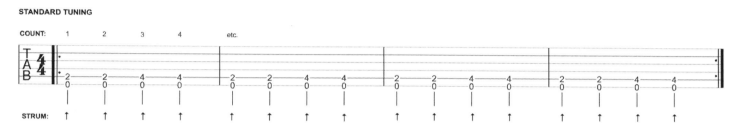

STRUMMING (1:15–1:00)

As you might have guessed, we're going to utilize quarter notes in today's strumming exercise, as well. Sticking with our open E and A chords, strum the entire exercise with downstrokes, shifting between chords every two beats. If you get tired of E and A, feel free to incorporate some of the other chords we've worked on so far this week. For example, you could try C and Am or Em and G, among other options.

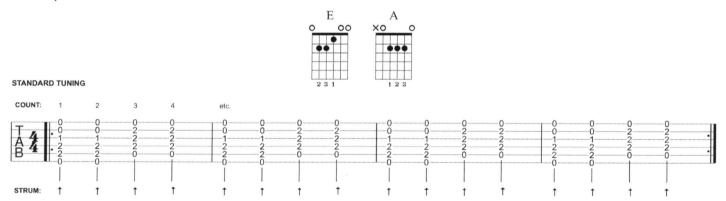

SINGLE-NOTE PICKING (1:00–0:45)

Now let's arpeggiate the E and A chords in a quarter-note rhythm. As recommended in the previous section, once you feel comfortable picking these two chords, you can try substituting other chords, as well. It's a good idea to get used to arpeggiating as many chords as possible, but only if you feel up to the task. At this point, you've got plenty on your plate, so the other chords can wait.

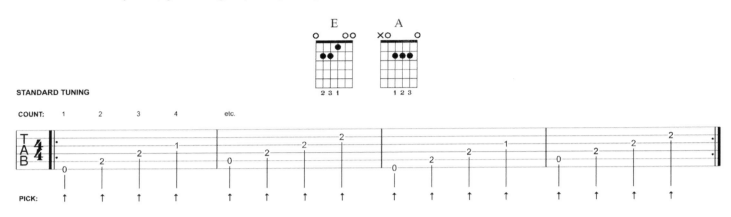

FINGERPICKING (0:45–0:30)

Our trusty *p–i–m–a* fingerpicking pattern makes yet another appearance. As before, keep your index *(i)*, middle *(m)*, and ring *(a)* fingers paired with strings 4, 3, and 2, respectively, while the thumb moves freely between strings 6 and 5 as the chords change. We want the notes of each chord to ring out, so reapply the picking fingers only after switching to the next chord. This will help to dampen the strings and eliminate unwanted noise.

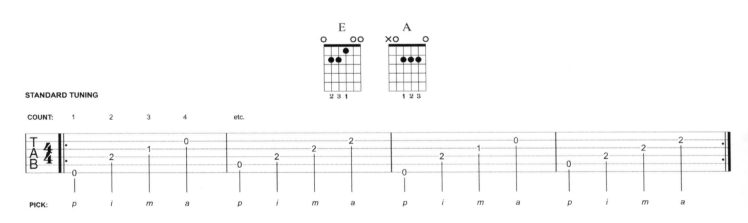

CHORD PROGRESSION (0:30–0:15)

In this next example, we're going to stray from our major and minor chords in favor of dominant 7th voicings. These types of chords are found in just about every style of music, from jazz and blues to country and funk.

Without getting too deep into the music-theory weeds, a dominant 7th chord contains four notes, while major and minor triads (the chords we've been studying up to this point) are comprised of three notes. Also, dominant 7th chords, known simply as "7th chords," are neither major nor minor; instead, they fall somewhere in between, with characteristics of both.

The E7 chord below should look *very* familiar because it's the same shape as the A chord from last week (in Open E tuning). Meanwhile, the A7 chord is similar to the regular A chord, but now we're fretting with just the middle (string 4) and ring (string 2) fingers and letting string 3 ring open.

The real challenge in this exercise is the B7 chord, particularly the note on string 1, which is played with the pinky. In addition to fretting challenges, perhaps the most difficult part of this chord is getting the 2nd string to ring out while being sandwiched between fretted pitches on strings 1 and 3. If you struggle with this chord initially, go ahead and strip it back to just the three lowest pitches (strings 5–3) until you can play the entire voicing cleanly.

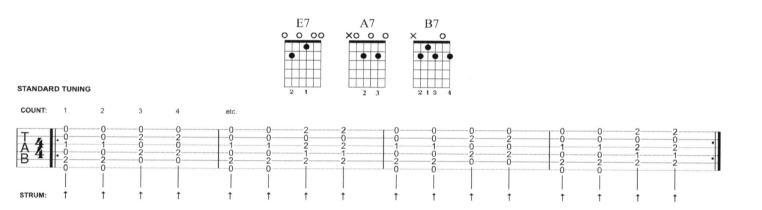

SCALE (0:15–0:00)

After spending a couple of days learning the C major scale, we're going to turn our attention to its relative minor, A minor. These two scales are "relative" because they share the exact same notes; the only difference is which note is considered the root. Since we already know the C major scale, this makes learning A minor relatively easy.

Instead of starting on the C note at fret 8 of string 6, we're going to start on the A note at fret 5, the root of the A minor scale. You'll also notice that the scale ends on fret 5 of string 1, which is also an A note, only it's two octaves higher than our starting note. Use alternate picking throughout, like you did for the major scale, and take it slow (50–60 BPM) and steady, gradually increasing your speed as you get more and more comfortable.

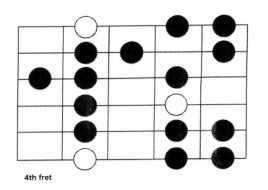

4th fret

STANDARD TUNING

COUNT: 1   2   3   4   etc.

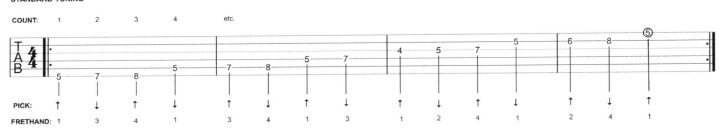

PICK: ↑   ↓   ↑   ↓   ↑   ↓   ↑   ↓   ↑   ↓   ↑   ↓   ↑   ↓   ↑

FRETHAND: 1   3   4   1   3   4   1   3   1   2   4   1   2   4   1

BLUES SHUFFLE (1:30–1:15)

In today's shuffle, we're going to continue our trend of subdividing the beat, playing eighth notes exclusively. We're also going to speed up the transitions between the index (fret 2) and ring (fret 4) fingers, which now occur on *every* beat. For more power and pick control, use downstrokes throughout.

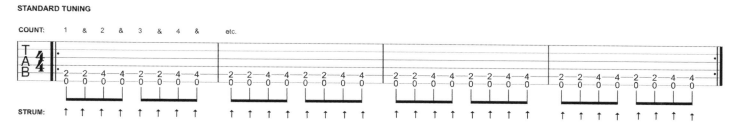

STRUMMING (1:15–1:00)

Eighth notes are our rhythm of choice in this exercise, as well. However, unlike our previous example, we're going to implement alternate strumming. We've used alternate strumming before, so it should feel familiar, but changing chords cleanly at this speed will take some patience. One trick—and every guitarists uses it—is to strum open strings on the last eighth note of each chord change—in our case, the "and" (upbeat) of beats 2 and 4. The sonic effect is negligible, especially at faster tempos, and it's really helpful when trying to "make the changes."

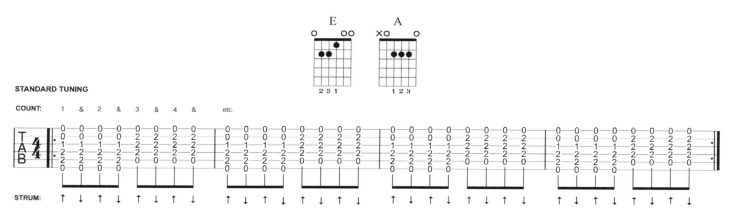

SINGLE-NOTE PICKING (1:00–0:45)

Now let's try picking our E and A chord changes in the eighth-note rhythm. As we've done before, use the open 5th string to your advantage; that is, as you change from E to A, let the open string afford you a little more time to get your index, middle, and ring fingers into place for the A chord. In other words, the A chord doesn't need to be fully voiced before plucking the open A (5th) string.

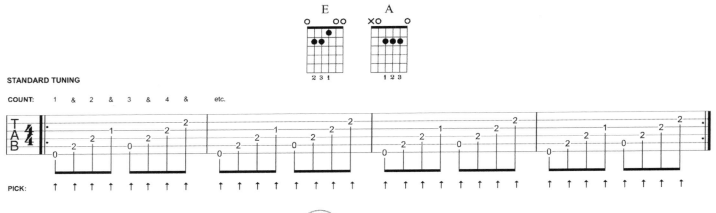

FINGERPICKING (0:45–0:30)

We're going to use the *p–i–m–a* picking pattern once again, but the chords are changing at a faster clip compared to yesterday's exercise. As before, keep your index *(i)*, middle *(m)*, and ring *(a)* fingers paired with strings 4, 3, and 2, respectively, while the thumb *(p)* bounces back and forth between string 6 and string 5.

Notice that the E chord change ends with an open string (string 2), and the A chord *begins* with an open string (string 5). Again, use these open strings to your advantage when switching between chords. For example, once you strike the open 2nd string on the "and" of beat 2, go ahead and start transitioning your fret-hand fingers to the A chord (beat 3).

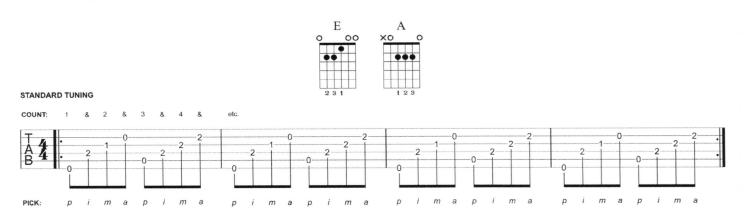

CHORD PROGRESSION (0:30–0:15)

In this exercise, we're going to take a look at a new chord progression, Cadd9–G–D, and a popular rhythm-guitar technique, *chord embellishment.* You might be thinking, "It looks like there are more than three chords in this progression. What about Dsus4 and Dsus2?" Well, that's a good question. Here's the short answer: Dsus4 and Dsus2 are simply *embellishments* of the D chord. Notice how the lower portion of the D chord (strings 2–4) stays intact while string 1 moves from fret 3 to fret 2 (measure 2), and from open to fret 2 (measure 4). This is an example of the aforementioned *chord embellishment,* also know as *ornamentation.* Even though we're shifting between different version of a D chord, the underlying harmony is still just D.

50

You may have noticed that Cadd9, G, and Dsus4 all share common notes—specifically, strings 2–1 (by the way, this is an alternate version of the G chord that we used previously). Therefore, as we change between these three chords, we can leave the ring and pinky fingers planted on strings 2 and 1, respectively, moving only our index and middle fingers to voice each new chord. Similarly, for the D, Dsus4, and Dsus2 chords, keep your index and ring fingers affixed to strings 3 and 2, respectively, while using your pinky and middle fingers to switch between notes on string 1.

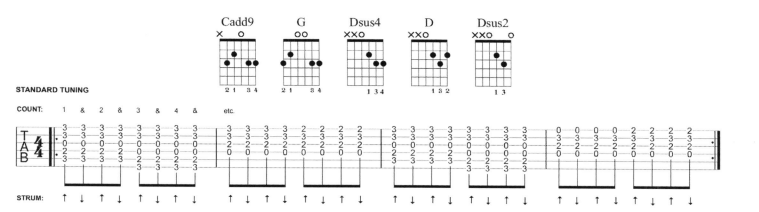

SCALE (0:15–0:00)

Today's pattern is the descending version of the A minor scale we learned yesterday. Start the pattern with a downstroke, using alternate picking throughout. If this picking pattern starts to feel comfortable, you can switch things up and begin with an upstroke, thereby reversing the direction of all of the subsequent pick attacks. As you know, some fret-hand shifting is involved, so be sure to follow the suggested fingerings, which are notated below the tab staff.

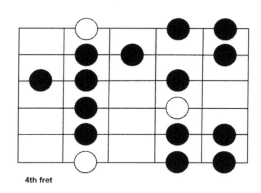

4th fret

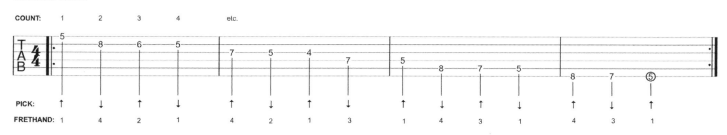

BLUES SHUFFLE (1:30–1:15)

In today's shuffle, we're going to increase the movement along string 5 to include the note at fret 5, D. Although I recommend using a combination of your index (fret 2), ring (fret 4), and pinky (fret 5) fingers, if the pinky stretch is too difficult at first, feel free to slide the ring finger back and forth between frets 4 and 5.

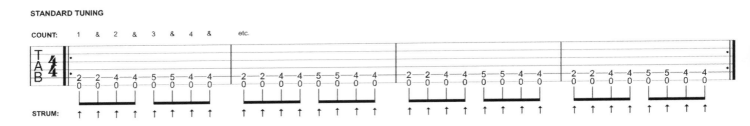

STRUMMING (1:15–1:00)

This exercise is a continuation of yesterday's figure, but we're going to add a third chord (G) to the festivities, turning our E–A progression into E–G–A–E. With the chords changing at this clip, don't be afraid to use the "open string" trick—in fact, I recommend it. Here's a refresher: on the "and" (upbeat) of beats 2 and 4, release the chord and allow your pick to strum open strings on the upstroke. The effect is negligible, particularly with certain chord progressions, including this one.

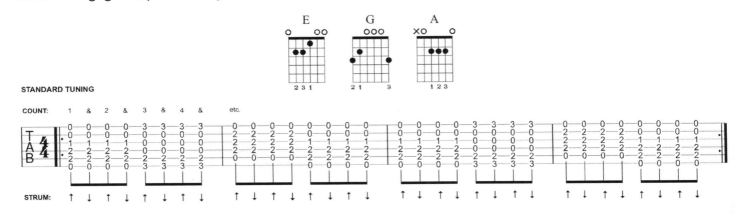

SINGLE-NOTE PICKING (1:00–0:45)

Now let's try picking our new E–G–A–E progression. Once again, we're going to arpeggiate all of the chords in ascending fashion. When moving from G to A, notice all of the open strings available to assist with making these changes. The open 4th and 3rd strings at the tail end of the G chord (beat 4 of measures 1 and 3) provide ample time to start transitioning the fret hand to the A chord. In certain keys, open strings can be a guitar player's best friend!

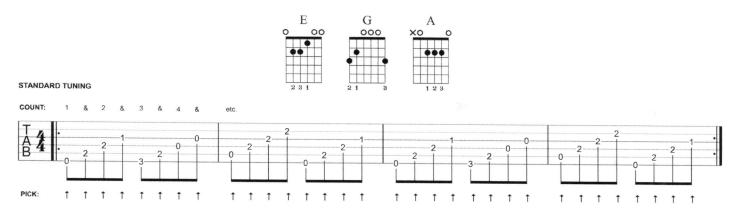

FINGERPICKING (0:45–0:30)

The addition of the G chord to our (previously) two-chord progression results in a bit of a different fingerpicking pattern. Instead of alternating between strings 6 and 5 for each chord change, the thumb now stays on string 6 for two chords, moves to string 5 for the A chord at the top of measure 2 (and measure 4), and returns to string 6 for the second iteration of the E chord. This change may seem minor but, after getting used to moving the thumb to a new string with each chord change, it will throw you off a bit, so take it slow at first.

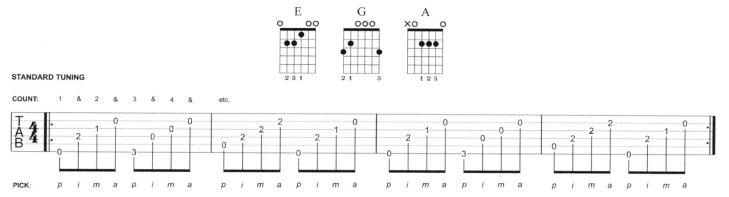

CHORD PROGRESSION (0:30–0:15)

This exercise will accomplish two thing: First, the B chord used here, Bsus4, will get your fret hand acclimated to a shape that will become *barre chords* in tomorrow's exercise. Second, you'll get your first taste of open-string "drones," a popular technique in modern music. If you look closely at the chord voicings below, you'll notice that each one contains open 1st and 2nd strings. Drones add resonance to progressions, as well as a sense of continuity.

When shifting from Asus2 to E, simply shift the middle and ring fingers down one string set (3–4 to 4–5) and add the index finger to fret 1 of string 3. Also, when moving from Bsus4 to Asus2, rather than going back to the original Asus2 fingering, you could instead keep your ring and pinky fingers affixed to strings 4 and 3, respectively, sliding them from fret 4 to fret 2 (and removing the index finger). Of course, the Asus2-to-E change would now be a bit more challenging, but experiment with both strategies and use which one you like best.

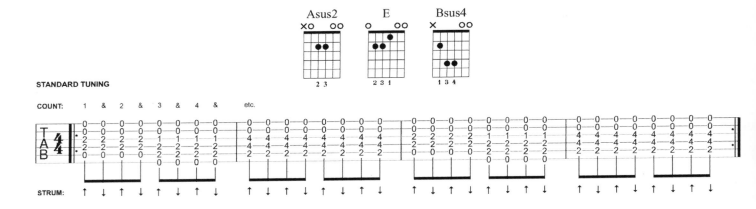

SCALE (0:15–0:00)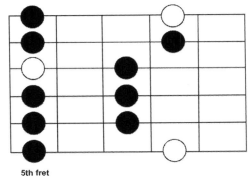

The C major (C–D–E–F–G–A–B) and A minor (A–B–C–D–E–F–G) scales we've learned up to this point have contained seven notes. Now, we're going to turn our attention to their five-note counterparts, C major pentatonic (C–D–E–G–A) and A minor pentatonic (A–C–D–E–G). These two scale are immensely popular in nearly all types of music, from rock and country to blues and jazz, so getting to know them intimately is strongly advised.

Here, we're going to focus on C major pentatonic (tomorrow we'll tackle A minor pentatonic). The pattern below is played in the same neck position as the C major pattern we learned previously, but now there is one less note on four of the six strings. Since there are fewer notes to memorize, we're going to practice this "box" pattern in both ascending and descending order. Once again, use alternate picking throughout and be mindful of the suggested fingerings, which are located below the tab staff.

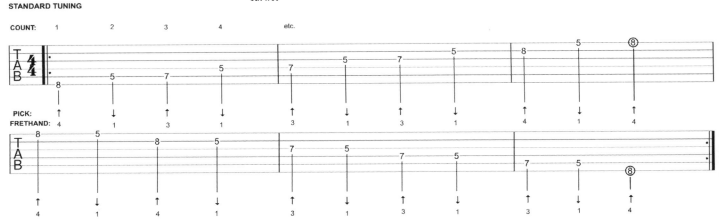

BLUES SHUFFLE (1:30–1:15)

This shuffle pattern is an extension of the one we worked on yesterday. The difference between the two is the movement that occurs on string 5. In the exercise below, the notes on string 5 bounce back and forth between frets 2, 4, and 5 on nearly every eight note, compared to every quarter note in yesterday's figure. Unlike yesterday's example, however, we can't cheat with our fret-hand fingers on this one. Since the exercise alternates pitches on nearly every beat, we have to keep the index finger in place at fret 2 at all times while reaching up to fret 4 with the ring finger and fret 5 with the pinky. In other words, we can't use the ring finger to float between those two higher frets—at least I don't advise it.

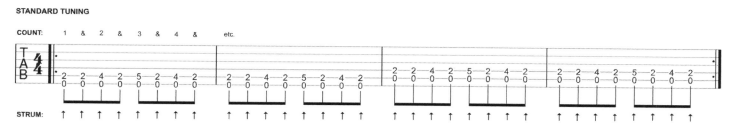

STRUMMING (1:15–1:00)

In the exercise below, the E–G–A–E progression from yesterday is given the 16th-note treatment. Remember to use the 16th-note counting prompt ("1 e & a, 2 e & a," etc.) and alternate strumming throughout. Once you've played through this example several times, at several different tempos, try strumming it entirely with downstrokes. This approach is a good way to add power to your picking hand, but be sure to practice it at a very slow tempo (40–45 BPM) at first.

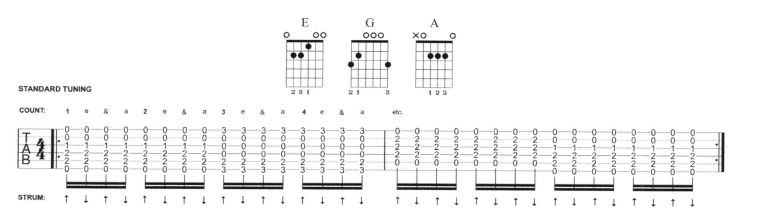

SINGLE-NOTE PICKING (1:00–0:45)

After several days of focusing exclusively on ascending arpeggios, today we're going to add some descending, or reverse, arpeggios. Pluck the ascending portion of each chord with four straight down-strokes, followed by four straight upstrokes for the descent. As mentioned last week, when you reach string 2, fight the urge to continue with an upstroke, and instead switch to an upstroke. The symmetry of four downstrokes and four upstrokes will help with your counting and timing.

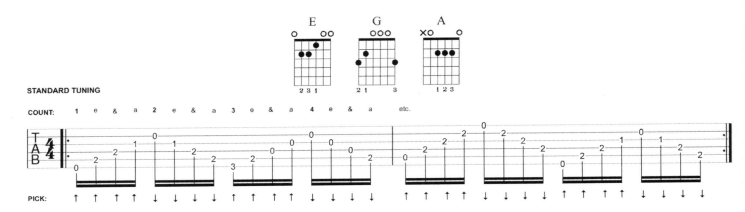

FINGERPICKING (0:45–0:30)

This fingerpicking exercise is similar to the one used back on Day 6. However, in this example, we have the added challenge of having to move the alternating thumb from strings 6 and 5 to strings 5 and 4 for the A chord, and then back to strings 6 and 5 for the return of the E chord.

The other challenge is having to switch between *p–i–m–a* (ascending) and *p–a–m–i* (descending) patterns while trying to alternate the thumb in time. To get a good handle on this exercise, listen to the audio demo to hear how it should sound—and feel free to play along if it's not too fast for you. And, as always, be sure to count!

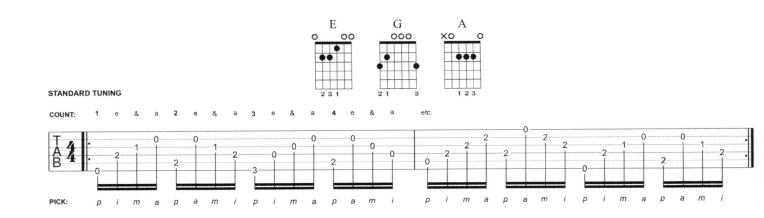

CHORD PROGRESSION (0:30–0:15)

I'm going to be honest: this chord progression is going to kick your butt. Hopefully, you won't let that deter you. One thing we haven't covered yet are *barre chords,* and for good reason—barre chords are difficult to play, particularly for beginners. Nonetheless, they're important, so we're going to dive right in.

Barre chords get their name from the fact that a fret-hand finger, typically the index or ring, is used to fret multiple notes on the same fret. The exercise below incorporates no fewer than four barre-chord types: sixth-string-root major shape (F), sixth-string-root minor shape (Gm), fifth-string-root major shape (C), and fifth-string-root minor shape (Dm). Since no open strings are used, we can move these shapes up or down the fretboard to play them in other keys. If any of the shapes give you trouble, feel free to exclude some of the higher strings; instead, try to get the lowest two or three strings to ring out, working towards the goal of getting all five or six strings to ring out cleanly.

Notice that, on the first beat of each chord, the root note is plucked individually before the entire chord is strummed in an eighth-and-two-16ths grouping. Plucking the root note like this is a good way to re-inforce the bass movement of the chords, particularly if you're playing solo or accompanying a vocalist without a bass player present.

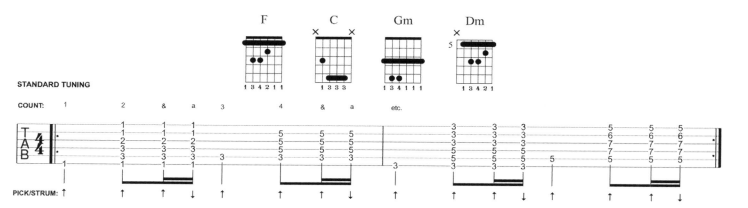

SCALE (0:15–0:00)

This scale, A minor pentatonic, is the relative minor of C major pentatonic—that is, both scales share the exact same notes and, therefore, the same pattern. This relationship is the same as the relationship between the seven-note C major and A minor scales, only we're dealing with fewer notes.

Instead of starting on the eighth-fret C note, we'll be starting from the A note at fret 5, which is the root of our new scale. As you play the pattern, focus on this note and the other root notes (white dots in the neck diagram), striving to hear them as "home base." Hearing A as the root instead of C is a challenge, especially after practicing the C major pentatonic scale just yesterday, but over time, you'll start to hear the difference between major and minor. As always, use alternate picking throughout.

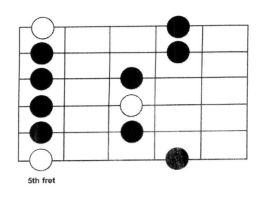

5th fret

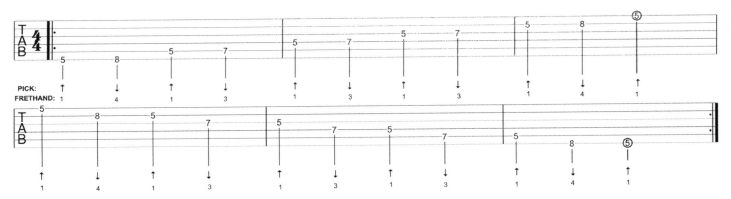

PUTTING IT ALL TOGETHER (1:30–0:00) 🔊

Congratulations on putting in two weeks of *hard* work! Now it's time to have a little fun!

Today, we're going to use the entire 90 minutes of practice time to review much of the material that we covered the previous 13 days. Below is an eight-measure example that features a C–G–Am–F progression (played twice) and includes such techniques as hammer-ons, pull-offs, slides, and muted strumming, music elements like quarter notes, eighth notes, and rests, and both open chords and barre chords.

Before you get started, listen to the audio demo to get a feel for all of the nuances of the passage. Then, attack the exercise in small chunks, working on measures 1–2 in isolation before adding measures 3–4, etc. Working in smaller increments is far less intimidating than trying to tackle the entire eight-bar example. And don't feel as though you have to have the entire eight-bar passage down cold when the timer goes off. Instead, just do the best you can do; you can always go back and review the material at a later date. In fact, I recommend revisiting any part of the book that gave you trouble, particularly in Week 2 (when you're in standard tuning). Good luck!

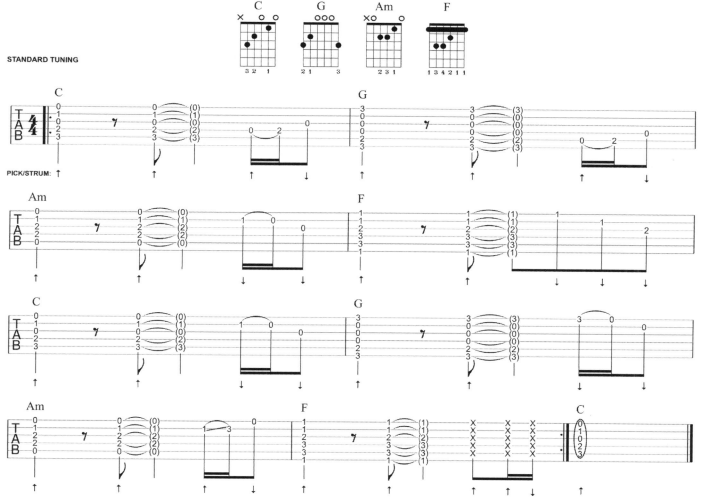

59

Printed in Great Britain
by Amazon